GLOBAL INDUSTRIES
UNCOVERED

THE PHARMACEUTICAL INDUSTRY

RICHARD SPILSBURY

WAYLAND

Published in paperback in 2014 by Wayland

Copyright © Wayland 2014

Wayland
338 Euston Road
London NW1 3BH

Wayland Australia
Level 17/207 Kent Street
Sydney NSW 2000

Series Editor: Claire Shanahan
Editor: Susie Brooks
Design: Rebecca Painter
Picture Researcher: Louise Edgeworth
Proofreader and Indexer: Cath Senker

British Library Cataloguing in Publication Data
Spilsbury, Richard, 1963-
   The pharmaceutical industry. -- (Global industries
   uncovered)
   1. Pharmaceutical industry--Juvenile literature.
   2. Industrial location--Juvenile literature.
   3. Globalization--Economic aspects--Juvenile
   literature.
   I. Title II. Series
338.4'76151-dc22

ISBN: 978 0 7502 8235 2

Picture acks: Cover and p38 © Joerg Boethling/Still Pictures;
1, 14, 35, 37 © AFP/Getty Images; 6, 13, 16, 17, 18, 26, 27
© Getty Images; 8 © Oliver Berg/epa/Corbis; 10 ©Itar–Tass/
UPPA/ Photoshot; 12 © Eye Ubiquitous/Photoshot; 19 Jeremy
Walker/Getty Images; 23 © Juda Ngwenya/Reuters/Corbis;
24   © EASI-Images/Roy Maconachie; 25 Gideon Mendel/Corbis
for UNICEF; 28 © Rex Features Ltd; 32 © Louise Gubb/Corbis;
33 © Jeff Christensen/Reuters/Corbis; 34 © Peter Turnley/ Corbis;
41 © Khalil Bendib, www.bendib.com

Printed in Malaysia

10 9 8 7 6 5 4 3 2 1

Wayland is a division of Hachette Children's Books,
an Hachette UK company.
www.hachette.co.uk

Contents

CASE STUDIES
UNCOVERED

Holly's family regularly use drugs, but not the illegal sorts. Her parents have a medicine cabinet containing headache tablets, indigestion remedies, cough mixtures and antiseptic creams. Her dad wears patches that help him to stop smoking and her gran has just finished a course of chemotherapy for breast cancer. Holly herself carries an inhaler for asthma attacks. Like the many people around the world who use medicinal drugs, or medicines, Holly and her family rely on the pharmaceutical industry. This is made up of a variety of companies that research, develop, test, manufacture and market medicines.

A global industry

The pharmaceutical industry is global. The biggest drug companies, such as GlaxoSmithKline and AstraZeneca, are giant, well-known and wealthy corporations called transnational companies (TNCs). TNCs have their headquarters in one country, usually a more developed country (MDC) such as the USA, but produce and market their medicines in several other global locations. For example, Johnson & Johnson is based in New Jersey, USA, but owns 250 companies spread over 57 countries. They make everything from band-aids and nappy cream to contact lenses and replacement hip joints – products that are sold in 175 countries worldwide.

There is a large variety of pharmaceutical products widely available for sale in MDCs.

Location, location

Different parts of the pharmaceutical industry are dotted around the world. Major drug companies have their headquarters in MDCs, because these are by far the highest spenders on pharmaceutical products. MDCs are also centres of the marketing and healthcare industries, which are closely linked to the pharmaceutical industry. Laboratories that develop new medicines are often located near MDC universities or health centres, where academic researchers work.

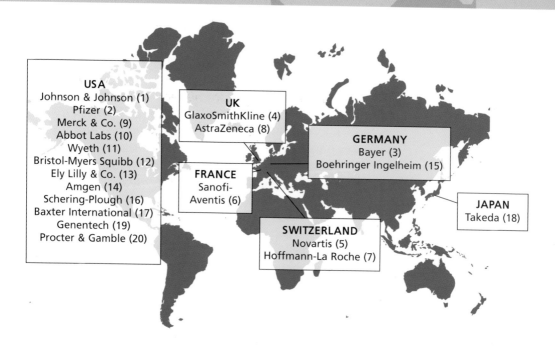

USA
Johnson & Johnson (1)
Pfizer (2)
Merck & Co. (9)
Abbot Labs (10)
Wyeth (11)
Bristol-Myers Squibb (12)
Ely Lilly & Co. (13)
Amgen (14)
Schering-Plough (16)
Baxter International (17)
Genentech (19)
Procter & Gamble (20)

UK
GlaxoSmithKline (4)
AstraZeneca (8)

GERMANY
Bayer (3)
Boehringer Ingelheim (15)

FRANCE
Sanofi-
Aventis (6)

JAPAN
Takeda (18)

SWITZERLAND
Novartis (5)
Hoffmann-La Roche (7)

Other factors affecting the location of the industry include natural and human resources. For example, pharmaceutical products are increasingly manufactured in less developed countries (LDCs) such as India, where labour is cheaper and where employment laws are less strict. Pharmaceutical companies are generally based near good transport routes, such as ports, railways, roads or airports. These allow them to distribute their products globally with ease. The companies are often located near big towns and cities, whose large populations provide employees and a market for the pharmaceutical goods.

This map shows the locations of the top 20 pharmaceutical TNCs, based on global earnings in 2006 (numbers in brackets show their rankings). Many of the top ten have headquarters in Europe, but overall most are based in the USA.

SPOTLIGHT

Globalisation: a shrinking world

Globalisation means that we live in a smaller, more connected, more interdependent world. Physically, the world is not smaller, but geographical distances seem less because it takes less time to travel to them or communicate between them. This has been made possible by improvements in technology. Mobile phones, the internet and low-cost flights are all examples of this. Global connections are faster, easier and cheaper, which means that industries use them more. It can be easy for those living in MDCs to take this for granted, but the technological revolution has not taken place at the same rate all over the world. As a result, some countries have benefited more than others from globalisation.

A big and wealthy industry

The pharmaceutical industry worldwide is very big and very rich. Annual sales of prescription drugs are worth over US$600 billion globally. This exceeds the GDP (total value of goods and services) of 90 per cent of all countries in the world. Almost half of all pharmaceutical products are bought in the USA, and most of these are produced by the big TNCs. These companies may have several billion-dollar brands, or particular products that each bring in over US$1 billion a year. The pharmaceutical industry provides work for millions of people – the five highest-earning US companies alone employ over 370,000. The biggest companies are at one end of the scale, but there are also numerous small companies. These have less money and fewer staff, but may have specialist knowledge or research skills. Big companies often buy up these smaller companies if they create a potentially successful drug or have desirable skills.

The pharmaceutical company Bayer has one of its biggest production facilities in an industrial zone in Leverkusen, Germany. The global success of products made here and in other sites, by Bayer, provides employment and wealth in western Germany.

Why is it global?

Over the last century, the pharmaceutical industry has grown in size and importance for two main reasons. First, there has been increased demand. World population has almost tripled since 1950. More people are able to access the media on anything from mobile phones to TVs, where they see marketing campaigns for pharmaceutical products. What is more, countries such as India and China are industrialising fast and their standard of living is gradually rising, so more people can afford pharmaceutical products now than in 1950.

Secondly, there are more pharmaceutical products on offer than in the past. Developments in medicine, such as advanced scanners and new surgical techniques, mean that more ailments can be identified and treated. Advances in computer technology, in laboratories to analyse chemicals for use in medicines and in factories to automate drug manufacture, allow drugs to be tested and produced more quickly than ever before.

In general, people are living longer and have a better quality of life. This is partly due to drugs which have eradicated some killer diseases, such as smallpox, and provided cures or relief for many other complaints.

SPOTLIGHT

Range of drugs

The pharmaceutical industry makes a wide range of medicines for different purposes. These include drugs for curing or treating symptoms of chronic (long-lasting and recurrent) illnesses such as Alzheimer's, and infectious (fast-spreading) diseases such as typhoid. They also include antibiotics for treating bacterial infections, sore-throat lozenges and contraceptive pills. However, globally people in different countries use different types of medicines. Up to half of all medicines used in China are traditional, or complementary, usually made of natural ingredients from plants and animals. These are not produced by the major pharmaceutical TNCs.

The pharmaceutical industry in the 20th century

1900s–1920s
The role of the pancreas and insulin is established in diabetes. Many vaccines against infectious diseases are developed.
1922 The company Eli Lilly start to sell insulin to treat diabetes.
1926 A vaccine for whooping cough is developed.

1930s–1940s
The widespread antibiotic properties of penicillin are discovered, and many antibiotics for infectious diseases are produced. Penicillin saves many lives and prevents many infected limbs being amputated during World War II.
1942 Merck mass-produce penicillin.
1945 Streptomycin antibiotic is found to be effective against tuberculosis.
1949 The first replacement lens is used to treat eye cataracts.

1950s–1960s
Many drugs are developed to calm people with psychiatric problems, including Valium, the most prescribed drug in history.
1952 Polio vaccine is developed.
1953 Sterling start to sell paracetamol in the USA. This becomes one of the most popular pain-relief drugs in history.
1960 The combined contraceptive pill goes on sale.
1963 Valium is approved for safety.

1970s–2000
Anti-cancer drugs and methods of using combinations of drugs to treat cancers are developed. A growing obesity problem starts a race to develop heart drugs. AIDS emerges as a significant world disease.
1972 A triple vaccine for measles, mumps and rubella (MMR) is introduced.
1978 The yew-tree bark extract taxol is found to be effective against cancers such as ovarian cancer.
1987 Prozac, the major anti-depressant drug, and AZT, the first AIDS drug, go on sale.
1992 Bristol-Myers Squibb exclusively sell taxol.
1995 Merck sell the first chicken pox vaccine.

This table shows a selective history of significant trends and discoveries in the global pharmaceutical industry, from 1900 to 2000.

New drugs

All new drugs have to be tested for the safety of the active ingredients, and to determine how much can be given to patients without causing harm. The usual process is to test first on animal tissue, then on live animals and finally on human volunteers, to check for any unwanted side-effects. Then the drug has a full clinical trial, when doctors monitor how patients treated with it react over months and years. Some drugs prove to be harmful during testing. In 2006, six volunteer testers suffered multiple organ failure during UK trials of a new drug.

The whole research and development system is very expensive, but the chemical formulae and manufacturing processes for new drugs are patented. This means that they cannot be used by other companies for around 14 years, so during this time the maker of a successful drug can make a large amount of money. When the patent ends, other drug makers around the world can use the formula to create cheaper versions, called generics. They can sell far more of the generics, generally at about 20 per cent of the cost of the patented version. This has a major effect on the sales of the original. For example, Eli Lilly, which produce the anti-depressant drug Prozac, experienced an 80 per cent global decline in sales within months of generic competitors entering the market.

Governing the industry

Thousands of different pharmaceutical products are developed each year, and it is in the interest of pharmaceutical companies to start selling them around the world to recover some of the money spent on research and testing. The industry is governed by independent organisations, to confirm to the public that the products are

Testing and manufacturing conditions are tightly regulated in most pharmaceutical facilities to ensure safety for workers and for users of medicines.

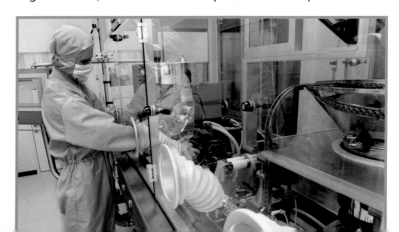

safe to use and have the health benefits they claim before sales begin. The organisations may be national, such as the US Food and Drug Administration (FDA), or international, such as the World Health Organisation (WHO), which governs global drug safety and availability. They may work with charities including Médecins sans Frontières (MSF) and UNICEF, which help to distribute drugs to some of the people in LDCs who need but cannot afford them. Other bodies, such as the Pharmaceutical Industry Competitiveness Task Force (UK), regulate the price of drugs to check consumers are paying a fair price.

SPOTLIGHT

Ideas for drugs

Many new ideas for drugs are based on natural remedies. Aspirin, for example, was developed from willow bark, an ancient cure for fever used in many global cultures. Others are discovered accidentally. In 1956, the Hoffmann-La Roche company created a new drug to fight tuberculosis, an infectious disease. However, the drug made patients feel happy, so it was used as the first anti-depressant drug.

Drug-testing process

Laboratory stage
Tissue samples
Computer simulation
Other *in-vitro* (outside the body) tests

Animal testing
Mainly rodents
Tests for toxicity (harmful effects)

MHRA and ethical bodies
Drug cleared for human testing

Human testing
Phase 1: Healthy volunteers
Testing for safety, side-effects

Phase 2: Selected people with relevant illness
Testing for effectiveness, side-effects

Phase 3: Large number of people with relevant illness
Testing for full information about the drug

Drug licensed
Phase 4: Wider testing against other drugs, testing for further side-effects and long-term risks and benefits

The stages in testing drugs are carefully governed. For example, the Medical and Healthcare products Regulatory Authority (MHRA) in the UK scrutinises results of animal testing to decide whether a new drug may harm human testers. They have to make ethical decisions balancing the pros of the drug in treating patients and the cons of risks to volunteer testers.

The pharmaceutical industry has a complex global structure. It is interdependent with a range of other industries, and there are also interdependencies between the many different businesses making up the pharmaceutical industry itself. Pharmaceuticals affect and are affected by a broad range of environmental, economic and social factors. These can have an impact on a local, national or global scale.

Tennis player Serena Williams receives medical attention on court. The treatment of sports injuries provides a regular market for the pharmaceutical industry. In return, many global pharmaceutical companies sponsor sporting events.

Interdependence of industries

There is close interdependence between the pharmaceutical industry and the healthcare and beauty industries that use its products. For example, national healthcare systems, such as the UK National Health Service (NHS), buy vast quantities of pharmaceutical products for use in hospitals and for surgery prescriptions. There is also some interdependence with industries such as tourism and sport, in which people are exposed to health risks. Sports people routinely get injured and tourists may need vaccinations to travel abroad.

Interdependencies within the pharmaceutical industry include competition between the thousands of drug companies. They may compete to sell different products containing the same active ingredients that treat the same conditions in very slightly different ways. Many businesses diversify, or increase the variety of products they offer. Some pharmaceutical companies diversify into non-medical products. For example, Procter & Gamble's brands include everything from osteoporosis drugs to batteries, razors and fabric softeners. Companies do this to widen overall sales to the general public rather than just medicine-users, and to get their name well known by a wider range of shoppers. The diversification can widen the global spread of companies.

Increasing demand

The demand for pharmaceutical products is affected by a variety of human processes. Population movement or trade can increase the spread of infectious diseases and the need for medicines. For example, leprosy and tuberculosis originated in East Africa and were spread to Europe by explorers and then to West Africa, the USA and other regions by the slave trade in the 18th and 19th centuries. Diet also affects medicine demand. People eating high-calorie diets and doing little exercise become obese and develop heart problems, while those on poor diets may become malnourished and unable to fight disease.

In many places, the demand for medicines cannot be met because pharmaceutical products are not available. On average, governments in MDCs spend over 100 times more on healthcare than countries in Africa. Some people, such as those living in remote mountain communities in Nepal, are physically cut off from places where they might obtain medicines. But the bigger problems of poverty and poor education mean that many people in LDCs just can't afford or do not know about many pharmaceutical products.

The financial crisis of 2007 onwards caused many people to lose their jobs and homes. The pools outside empty, repossessed houses in warm parts of the USA proved to be ideal breeding grounds for mosquitoes. This led to a rise in cases of West Nile Fever (spread by the insects) and higher demand for drugs to treat the disease.

SPOTLIGHT

Unsafe products

Some drugs and other products of the pharmaceutical industry are unsafe to use and are a growing problem in both LDCs and MDCs. Fakes, or counterfeit drugs, are intentionally poor copies of drugs that contain dangerous or no active ingredients. They are made cheaply by criminals to sell in place of genuine drugs. Substandard drugs are unsafe as they are accidentally contaminated by other chemicals while being made, often as a result of poor regulation of manufacture. For example, in 2008, batches of the blood thinner heparin, made in China, were contaminated with an industrial chemical. It is suspected that the drug killed 81 people in the USA and triggered allergic reactions in hundreds worldwide.

Responding to needs

The pharmaceutical industry benefits people in many ways, most notably by curing illnesses and saving lives. However, needs differ according to individuals, cultures and the times. For example, a malnourished baby at a health centre in Somalia may need a simple cure for diarrhoea in order to live, whereas some doctors prescribe expensive Botox treatment for people in MDCs who claim their quality of life is affected by facial wrinkles.

The industry also responds to the need for jobs. The location of those jobs can vary depending on the cost of wages and the economic climate. For example, Indian states compete with each other by offering low taxes and subsidies to encourage drug companies to set up plants and research facilities as they offer jobs and generate wealth for their regions. Large pharmaceutical companies are wealthy businesses, so they are also major sponsors of and donors to anything from education or healthcare centres to globally important arts and sports events. For example, the Takeda pharmaceutical company of Japan sponsors tours by the London Symphony Orchestra around the globe.

Marketing medicines

Marketing of drugs varies across the world. In the UK, drug companies cannot advertise the prescription medicines they make, but they can provide disease awareness information, such as the dangers of heart disease and how drugs can

The provision of pharmaceutical products by a village clinic in Somalia, run by the charity MSF, offers a lifeline to poor people in a war-ravaged country with little access to medicine.

help, to patients under their company name. In the USA, companies can market prescription drug brands and make claims about their benefits. This leads to many consumers demanding particular brands from their doctors, when cheaper generics would work just as well. Not surprisingly, the industry overall spends far less on marketing in LDCs, where fewer products will be sold, than in MDCs.

> *If I'm a manufacturer and I can change one molecule and get another twenty years of patent rights, and convince physicians to prescribe and consumers to demand... weekly Prozac instead of daily Prozac, just as my patent expires, then why would I be spending money on a lot less certain endeavour, which is looking for brand-new drugs?*

Dr Sharon Levine, Kaiser Permanente Medical Group, 2002

There is generally tight regulation of pharmaceutical advertising; for example, it is necessary to mention possible side-effects and how the drugs were tested. However, the pharmaceutical industry sometimes claims medicines are much more useful than they really are. Doctors suggest that some pharmaceutical companies have even invented and advertised distinct conditions such as an overactive bladder, which may just be a symptom of other treatable bladder problems, in order to sell their products. The regulation of marketing is weakest in the growing beauty sector of the industry. For example, companies may make claims for anti-ageing creams that have been tested on far fewer people than a drug would require.

SPOTLIGHT

Innovation or marketing?

Many of the new drugs produced each year are 'me-too' drugs that are basically copies of market leaders. In 2002, 78 drugs were approved by the FDA, but only 17 contained new active ingredients. Just seven of these were classified by the FDA as improvements on older drugs. Research in 2012 suggested that the global pharmaceutical industry spends twice as much on marketing drugs as it does on research. Should the drug companies be innovating more to cure more illnesses?

Ways of marketing

A third of all US pharmaceutical marketing involves approaching doctors or nurses one-to-one. Representatives visit to talk about new products and may give out gifts ranging from cookies to calendars, pens and clocks with the name of the pharmaceutical company or drug branded on them. Company adverts appear in newspapers, magazines and on the TV and internet. Companies sponsor doctors to mention their products in lectures or in journal articles. Many pharmaceutical companies also employ political lobbyists, who promote the industry to politicians, and donate to political parties in the hope that they might influence future funding or laws governing the industry. For example, in the US presidential elections of 2008, Barack Obama's campaign received well over US$500,000 from the pharmaceutical industry. Drug companies were concerned that Obama would try to make prescription drugs cheaper for more people without health insurance and therefore affect the companies' profits.

Political donations by pharmaceutical companies, like those from any other industry, are a normal source of funding for US election campaigns and are closely regulated. Here, Barack Obama campaigns for people to vote for his as president in the US elections of 2008

Physical processes

The locations where medicines are produced depend partly on physical resources. For example, NaturNorth make anti-cancer drugs from birch bark, and in 2006 set up a major bark-processing plant near Duluth, USA, where the climate naturally suits the growth of birch trees. But physical processes affect the pharmaceutical industry in other ways, too. Natural disasters such as floods and landslides can contaminate water supplies and cause water-borne diseases such as cholera to spread, increasing the demand for medicines. Seasonal changes in weather can also increase demand. For example, in the UK flu jabs are given out to the elderly before cold winters.

Most scientists agree that global warming is gradually changing world climates. This is already altering the distribution of disease-carrying organisms such as ticks. For example, unusually warm winters in Russia, the USA and Japan have all seen a rise in cases of Lyme disease – an illness carried by ticks, which would normally die off during very cold spells. Sufferers experience problems with the nervous system and joints, which can only be treated with antibiotics.

A 78-year-old woman receives a flu jab, offered for free by the city of Chicago, USA, in autumn 2006. Her jab was one of around 100 million bought by the US government from vaccine makers, to protect people against a winter epidemic.

SPOTLIGHT

Web pharmacies

There are hundreds of websites selling prescription drugs. Internet sales of these medicines exceeded US$75 billion in 2012. Demand has risen in countries such as the USA, where people have to pay for their healthcare, and many cannot afford sufficient health insurance to cover the cost. Until about 2005, many Americans bought from Canadian websites, but now they use businesses based as far away as India, Russia and South Africa, where drugs are even cheaper. The problem with some internet pharmacies is that they sell genuine medicines without requiring prescriptions, which means that consumers may take the wrong doses or the wrong medicines. The pharmacies also sell counterfeit drugs, either because they are cheaper to buy or else their suppliers substitute them for genuine drugs. In Europe, an estimated 62 per cent of medicines sold online are fake.

Environmental interaction

The pharmaceutical industry, like any other industry, interacts with the global environment. For example, poachers kill rare tigers to sell their body parts for use in Chinese traditional medicines. Another effect is pollution, including that caused by some strong anti-cancer drugs, which pass through patients' urine and cannot easily be removed during water purification. The drugs can have harmful effects on people who drink the water. Some companies are trying to reverse the negative effects of their products, partly to benefit themselves. For example, an estimated 25 per cent of active ingredients in drugs today are obtained from rainforest plants, including various cancer treatments. Since 1998, the US TNC Bristol-Myers Squibb has invested in forest conservation in Surinam. In return the company receives shared benefit, with the Surinamese government, from any medicines derived from Surinamese rainforest plants.

Scientists collect insects as part of a project, funded by Merck pharmaceutical company, to identify potential raw ingredients for drugs from Costa Rican rainforest flora and fauna.

The sustainable alternative

Every industry is increasingly aware of sustainability, or the ways in which it can limit its impact on the environment by using fewer natural resources. Most businesses in the pharmaceutical industry are trying to reduce the amount of energy used in manufacturing drugs and the packaging around their products. For example, under the US government's WasteWise program, Allergan Inc. has reduced the weight of cardboard and plastic used to pack its products, such as lens implants, by hundreds of tonnes each year. Sanofi-Aventis's ECOVAL committee regularly assesses the environmental impacts of making its top 23 drugs, which represent over two-thirds of its sales. One way the company reduces its impact is by recycling the water used for processing drugs in its factories.

The future of the pharmaceutical industry

There are several developing trends that will affect the pharmaceutical industry in future decades. By 2025, more than a billion people worldwide will be over 60, and older people generally need more medicines than younger people. At the same time, world financial problems are limiting the amount that governments can spend on healthcare and that drug companies can spend on research and development. The pharmaceutical industry will also lose revenue from best-selling brands, which together contributed over US$157 billion in revenue in 2005, because they are becoming generic by 2015. The challenge for the pharmaceutical industry is to continually develop new medicines that the public will buy to meet their future health demands.

SPOTLIGHT

New treatments

Every year there are new medicines. For example, in 2008, US researchers created a special powder called extracellular matrix, which made a severed finger regrow on its hand. This regeneration technology could change the need for medicine to deal with the effects of tissue damage such as burns or cancer damage. There are also new ways to deliver medication to people, such as a form of insulin from Pfizer that people with diabetes can inhale rather than inject. In future, many pharmaceutical companies hope to be able to supply personalised medication. The plan is to analyse the genes of individual patients to produce specific drugs that work for them.

The pharmaceutical industry of the future faces a challenge to maintain its profits and meet public demands while at the same time becoming more sustainable, for example by polluting less than today.

HIV/AIDS is the world's most deadly infectious disease. In southern Africa, HIV/AIDS is the leading cause of death, and globally it is the fourth-greatest killer. The spread of the disease and the numbers of deaths varies between MDCs and LDCs, owing to the differing availability of effective drug treatments and education about preventing the disease. These differences are largely related to financial resources. If the global pharmaceutical industry has developed treatments to slow the disease, why do 70 per cent of HIV/AIDS sufferers still not have access to them?

HIV to AIDS

The Human Immunodeficiency Virus (HIV) destroys or damages cells in the immune system. The patient's immune system gets weaker and he or she gradually loses the ability to fight infections, such as colds. Some people then develop AIDS (Acquired Immune Deficiency Syndrome), which is a group of rare illnesses that shut down the immune system completely. AIDS victims often die within a year, from conditions such as pneumonia, diarrhoea or tumours.

HIV/AIDS is a far bigger problem in many LDCs than in MDCs. For example, in 2013, around 0.5 per cent of the population aged 15–49 in the UK or USA were infected with HIV. In Swaziland, Lesotho and Botswana in southern Africa, the figure was approximately 25 per cent.

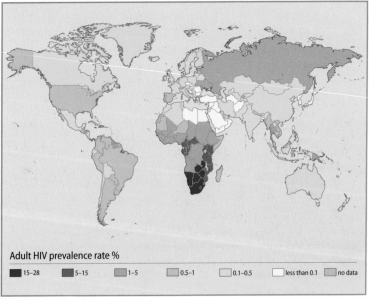

Adult HIV prevalence rate %

15–28   5–15   1–5   0.5–1   0.1–0.5   less than 0.1   no data

Source: UNAIDS, 2008

The HIV virus (or more specifically, retrovirus) spreads in body fluids from infected people during sexual intercourse and injecting illegal drugs, but also during breast-feeding and blood transfusions, or blood replacement necessary in treating blood disorders such as haemophilia. There is no known cure or vaccine for HIV/AIDS, but anti-retroviral (ARV) drugs such as AZT, often given in combination with other drugs to work more effectively, can slow the weakening of the immune system and prevent AIDS from developing.

Treatment in MDCs

Anti-retrovirals are expensive drugs, typically costing thousands of dollars a year in MDCs. The cost of dealing with HIV/AIDS is not only the cost of ARVs. It also includes a large team of specialists, such as doctors, nurses, blood testers, to diagnose and treat illness and counsellors to help people come to terms with a potentially fatal disease, as well as healthcare facilities and government campaigns to stop the spread of the disease. Wealthy MDC countries generally have the money to provide and pay for all of this. In most MDCS, such as the UK, HIV treatment is via the NHS. However, in the USA, individuals may have to pay directly or via health insurance plans. An infected individual's ability to stay healthy in the USA depends on what he or she can afford.

SPOTLIGHT

Where you live

There are differences between countries, and regions within them, in the treatments or facilities available to counter HIV/AIDS effects. For example, people who inject drugs are at particular risk, so some countries such as the Netherlands offer free clean needles to drug users to avoid reusing needles and spreading the disease. In Spain, where the government believes needle exchange promotes illegal drug use, around half of injecting drug users are HIV positive. Some people taking HIV medication suffer the side-effect of facial wasting, and in the UK only eight treatment centres offer effective treatment for this condition. Some people are excluded from treatment owing to where they live. This is an example of what is called postcode prescribing.

Treatment economics

In the 1980s to 1990s, ARV drugs were very expensive, so most people in LDCs could not afford treatment. For example, the ARV Stavudine, developed in 1998 by the US TNC Bristol-Myers Squibb, cost over US$8 for a day's treatment – far more than most African sufferers earned. In the late 1990s, South Africa passed a law enabling local companies to make cheaper generics of ARVs and allowing cheaper generics to be imported from countries such as Brazil, India and Thailand. Some of the world's leading drug companies, such as Bristol-Myers Squibb, were afraid these cheaper drugs would break into the market in MDCs. They claimed that their high drug prices were needed to fund research and development, so they tried to use international copyright law to stop South Africa making and distributing generics. This caused an international outcry, and TNCs were accused of trying to profit from the suffering of the poor. The drug companies dropped their challenge in 2001 and the move to generics slashed the cost of annual treatment from as much as US$15,000 per patient in the late 1990s to as little as US$150 in 2008.

South Africans protest on the streets during the 13th International AIDS conference in Durban, South Africa, 2000, to encourage drug companies to slash ARV prices.

SPOTLIGHT

Different drugs

Even though older ARVs are much cheaper than in the past, the newest, most effective treatments remain expensive because they are not widely available in LDCs. For example, the pharmaceutical company Abbott created an improved version of an ARV called Lopinavir/Ritonavir in 2005 that, unlike some other ARVs, is not affected by warm, damp, tropical conditions. Many tropical LDCs have the highest levels of HIV/AIDS, so this ARV would be especially useful. However, in 2006, Abbott's new ARV was not registered for sale in a single LDC in Africa. Is this because under international AIDS agreements, these countries are allowed to buy such essential medicines at low prices? By contrast, in Thailand and Guatemala, both LDCs that are not included in the AIDS agreements, Abbott is selling the ARV at over US$2,000 for a year's treatment. This amount is more than the average annual wage for a single person.

LDC challenges

Amongst the biggest challenges for HIV/AIDS treatment in LDCs is that many infected people do not seek diagnosis and those that are diagnosed with HIV do not always have uninterrupted courses of ARV drugs, so they progress more quickly to AIDS. These problems often stem from social factors, such as gender differences and a lack of education. For example, women may have less time to attend appointments than men because of the large amount of domestic work they have to carry out each day, and many families cannot afford education, so people do not fully understand when they risk catching the disease.

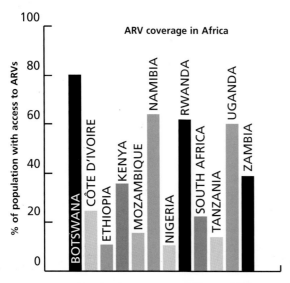

In Africa the ARV coverage, or availability of ARV, across a country varies from 80 per cent of Botswana down to just over 10 per cent in Nigeria.

SPOTLIGHT

Global black market in AIDS drugs

Pharmaceutical companies lose large amounts of possible revenue by selling ARVs cheaply in Africa. This loss is increased when criminals resell the cheap AIDS drugs at a huge profit in Europe and the USA illegally on the black market. In 2002, investigators working for GlaxoSmithKline discovered that a government official in Senegal, Africa, had stolen and sold £12 million worth of ARVs to Europeans via internet pharmacies. One drug, Combivir, sells for £340 a box in the UK but £33 in Africa to make it affordable. The smuggler was making several hundred pounds in profit on each box of African ARVs he sold to the pharmacies.

Migration of the virus

Many people from LDCs migrate to other countries. Some move to find better-paid work and others to escape troubled times, such as the extended civil wars in the Democratic Republic of Congo and Rwanda. A few move to MDCs. Some migrants have HIV, and migration can spread the virus. About 25 per cent of HIV infections in western Europe are among migrants from southern Africa, and African-born immigrants have the highest prevalence of HIV among all nationalities of immigrants. Some governments have taken action against the immigration of infected people. For example, in 2007, Australian prime minister John Howard called for a ban on any HIV-infected people being allowed to move to Australia. In Canada, foreigners applying for residency are tested and very likely to be refused if they are HIV-positive, owing to the possible healthcare costs for the country. People from MDCs also spread the virus through travel. For example, in 2007 around one-fifth of all new HIV infections reported in Europe were picked up on global travels to Africa, Latin America or the Caribbean.

Public information campaigns, such as this roadside sign in Sierra Leone, are important in educating people about HIV/AIDS.

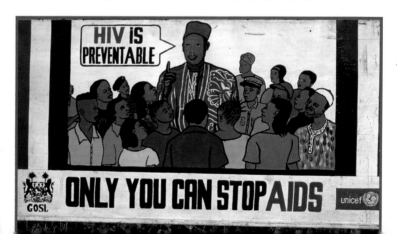

Political impacts

The distribution and availability of drugs for HIV/AIDS is also affected by national politics. Thabo Mbeki was president of South Africa from 1999 to 2008. In 2000, he declared that the AIDS epidemic was caused by poverty and malnutrition and not the HIV virus. He also declared that available drugs such as AZT were poisonous and dangerous. His policy has been directly blamed for 330,000 AIDS deaths in the country. After he left office in 2008, the UK government announced that it would give South Africa's new health minister £15 million to help combat AIDS there.

Since 2003, the USA has confronted the growing AIDS crisis in Africa with its President's Emergency Plan for AIDS Relief (Pepfar). By 2008, this scheme had spent US$15 billion on free ARVs, built clinics, helped increase drug coverage and lobbied drug companies to drop ARV patents. Pepfar has saved nearly 2 million lives and supports 10 million people affected by AIDS by providing food, education and housing. However, some people believe that in helping Africa, Pepfar has also favoured US drug companies too much, and might have helped even more people if the programme had supplied cheaper generic ARVs than expensive, big-name brands. In 2005, only 10 per cent of ARVs supplied were generics, largely because Pepfar approved very few for use.

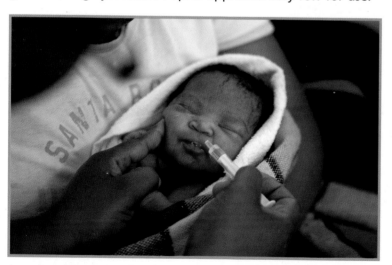

A newborn baby in Lesotho receives a dose of ARV to prevent her HIV-positive mother passing on the virus via her breastmilk. Initiatives including Pepfar are making this sort of treatment more widely available through southern Africa, but globally millions cannot access the best services and drugs to cope with HIV/AIDS.

PERSPECTIVES FOR DEBATE

"In 2003, only 50,000 Africans were on HIV antiretroviral drugs – and they had to pay for their own medicine. Today, 1.3 million are receiving medicines free of charge."

Bob Geldof, 2008

"It's simply unacceptable that we have to wait many years to use medicines that are commonly used in wealthy countries, if we get them at all."

Dr Moses Massaquoi, MSF, Malawi, 2006

Today, Pfizer is the world's largest pharmaceutical company. This giant TNC sells nearly US$50 billion-worth of pharmaceutical products each year. Pfizer's worldwide business began in the USA and grew by creating several billion-dollar brands that are in demand globally. It has also flourished by fighting competition from other drug companies and generics.

The beginnings

Pfizer started life in 1849 as a chemicals business in Brooklyn, New York, USA, selling drugs that kill worm parasites in animals and people. It grew from the late 19th century by making citric acid, used for example to preserve food and make cleaning products, and the antibiotic penicillin. The company spread by opening businesses in the UK, Belgium, Brazil and several other countries in the middle of the 20th century. It also started to make drugs in Italy and Mexico. Pfizer then moved its base to New York City, in order to be closer to US banks and other businesses that

In 2009, Pfizer took over its competitor Wyeth, at a cost of US$68 billion, to become the world's largest biopharmaceutical company. In the picture above, the chief executive officers of Pfizer (left) and Wyeth shake hands.

helped to finance its expansion. The major-selling drugs created by Pfizer scientists include their first billion-dollar drug Piroxicam, which stops tissue inflammations such as arthritis, and the anti-depressant Zoloft.

Acquiring brands

Pfizer expanded its range of products by buying up companies holding patents for possible best-selling drugs. In the 1980s, legislation was changed so that universities and small laboratories could patent their new discoveries. In many cases, research had been sponsored by the National Institutes of Health, a US government department. The rich TNCs then bought up these small companies and their exclusive rights to discoveries funded by public money. For example, the scientist who discovered Atorvastatin (see Spotlight), Bruce Roth, worked at the University of Rochester. The Warner-Lambert pharmaceutical company gave Roth a job and a big laboratory and team to develop the drug. Warner-Lambert agreed to share worldwide marketing of the drug's active ingredient, Lipitor, with Pfizer, which were especially good at marketing new drugs. They had a large team of sales representatives and medical expertise. Pfizer made sure Lipitor sold cheaper than its main competitor, Merck's Zocor, and was liked better by doctors. By 2000, Pfizer was big enough to buy Warner-Lambert and take over exclusive rights to Lipitor.

SPOTLIGHT

The blockbuster drug

Atorvastatin, the active ingredient in Pfizer's Lipitor, is the most valuable single drug in the world. This blockbuster drug generated annual sales of over US$10 billion each year from 2004 to 2008. The drug slows the body's production of LDL cholesterol, which can build up on the inner walls of blood vessels and lead to heart disease or strokes. The body only makes lots of LDL if people eat too much very fatty or sugary food. This is loosely an illness of MDCs, where people have inactive lifestyles and eat high-calorie diets. Today, the USA spends an estimated US$100 billion per year treating the effects of obesity. However, the future of Lipitor and its annual revenue for Pfizer is bleak. This drug is coming off patent in 2011 and will be replaced by cheaper, generic versions.

Blockbuster drugs such as Lipitor make up one-third of the total drug market.

Life after Lipitor

Pfizer has tried to maximise revenue from Lipitor in different ways while its patent lasts. For example, in 2005, Pfizer marketed Lipitor to women and people over 65, who generally buy more medicines than younger people. They claimed that taking the drug prevented future heart problems. There were no studies proving this, but as a result, many people bought the drug without needing to. When the drug's main competitor, Merck's Zocor, went out of patent in 2007, Pfizer launched a worldwide campaign against generic versions of Zocor. They based this on their own study showing increased heart problems when patients switched from Lipitor. Doctors were not convinced, carried on prescribing the much cheaper alternatives, and Lipitor sales dropped by 25 per cent in 2007.

Pfizer also developed Torcetrapib, another heart drug, as a successor to Lipitor. It was highly promising in laboratory tests, but disaster struck in clinical trials on 15,000 patients with heart problems. The death rate increased by 60 per cent in those who took Torcetrapib and Lipitor compared with those who took Lipitor alone. The drug was withdrawn and the US$1 billion it cost to develop was wasted.

Products are stacked high at a Pfizer distribution centre in Belgium. Global distribution centres and the transport industry are important for spreading Pfizer's products to pharmacies and healthcare providers, and then to its customers.

Global company

Today, Pfizer is located globally. It is still based in New York, where the team manages legal and financial aspects of the TNC and its employees. Pfizer's research headquarters in Groton, Connecticut, occupies a 65-hectare site containing the largest pharmaceutical research facility in the world. Research is carried out in six laboratories, four of which are in the USA, and each has its own research specialisms (see right). Worldwide, in 2009 Pfizer had 48 of its own factories and licensed others it did not own to make its products, too. Since the Torcetrapib failure, Pfizer has made several cost-cutting measures such as closing research laboratories in Japan, France and the USA in 2007 and 2008.

Future specialisms

In 2008, Pfizer decided to end new research on heart disease drugs and identified six high-priority areas for future research, including cancer, diabetes and Alzheimer's disease. Pfizer is sponsoring breast cancer research and awareness and researching new ways of testing. For example, it has developed a method of analysing hair strands for the likelihood of getting the disease, and through a nationwide survey on breast cancer care in the UK, discovered women were not getting the best long-term treatment. This could stimulate better care for cancer patients in future, while also confirming the association between the disease and the cancer-busting treatments that Pfizer produces.

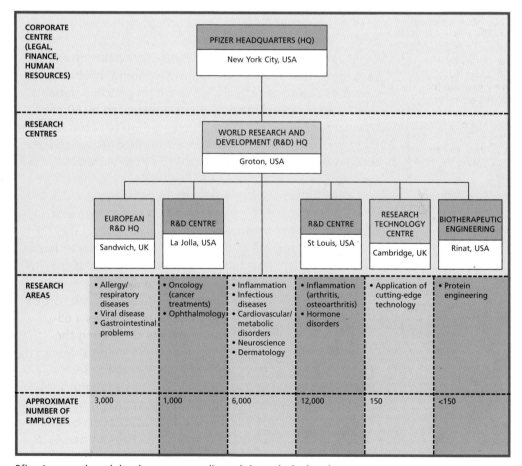

CORPORATE CENTRE (LEGAL, FINANCE, HUMAN RESOURCES)	PFIZER HEADQUARTERS (HQ) New York City, USA				
RESEARCH CENTRES	WORLD RESEARCH AND DEVELOPMENT (R&D) HQ Groton, USA				
	EUROPEAN R&D HQ Sandwich, UK	R&D CENTRE La Jolla, USA	R&D CENTRE St Louis, USA	RESEARCH TECHNOLOGY CENTRE Cambridge, UK	BIOTHERAPEUTIC ENGINEERING Rinat, USA
RESEARCH AREAS	• Allergy/ respiratory diseases • Viral disease • Gastrointestinal problems	• Oncology (cancer treatments) • Ophthalmology	• Inflammation • Infectious diseases • Cardiovascular/ metabolic disorders • Neuroscience • Dermatology	• Inflammation (arthritis, osteoarthritis) • Hormone disorders	• Application of cutting-edge technology	• Protein engineering
APPROXIMATE NUMBER OF EMPLOYEES	3,000	1,000	6,000	12,000	150	<150

Pfizer's research and development, coordinated through the headquarters at Groton, Connecticut, creates products at 48 Pfizer facilities and other facilities, making drugs for different companies.

Malaria is a global disease that kills about one million people each year and inflicts painful illness on hundreds of millions of others, mostly in LDCs. Pharmaceutical companies are coordinating their quest for more effective treatment, especially a vaccine against the disease, in association with charities and aid agencies worldwide.

Malaria spreads

Malaria is caused by the tiny, eyelash-shaped parasite Plasmodium. This organism reproduces and then erupts from red blood cells, provoking the immune system to release chemicals that cause chills, pain, fever, and even brain damage. Once people have the disease, fever usually recurs in episodes throughout their lives. Plasmodium gets into people when mosquitoes feed on human blood. The insects carry the infection from host to host. Types of mosquitoes that spread malaria live mostly in warm, wet tropical countries. These provide ideal conditions for mosquitoes, which breed by laying eggs in still water.

The spread of malaria is influenced by many geographical factors. For example, a 2009 study in Ethiopia showed that children living near man-made reservoirs, built to supply hydroelectric power, had seven times more malaria sickness bouts than those living further away. The disease also spreads when people migrate. For example, poor Thai farm workers who migrate into tropical forests to mine for gems, to make more money, catch malaria from the forest mosquitoes. They then carry the disease home when they return to farms after the mining work has finished.

Taking the medicine

The active ingredients chloroquine, mefloquine and artemisinin are some of the most common antimalarials. They work by building up in Plasmodium and preventing the parasite from damaging blood cells. There are problems with antimalarials. The drugs do not provide protection unless people take tablets every day or every week. Another big problem is resistance, when Plasmodium is no longer affected by antimalarials.

The research divisions of pharmaceutical companies commonly screen, or test out, thousands of new compounds each year to see how effectively they work on a whole range of conditions. They generally do not screen new compounds for antimalarial effectiveness. The reason is that it would take a long time to recover the money invested in research and development from the mostly poor people who have the disease. This is true for most tropical diseases, which occur largely in LDCs. Only 13 out of 1,223 new medicines marketed by major drug companies between 1975 and 1997 were developed for tropical diseases, according to Médecins Sans Frontiéres.

SPOTLIGHT

Wormwood cures

Artemisinin-based drugs are the most effective antimalarials. Artemisinin is obtained from the plant Artemisia, or wormwood, and because it cannot be produced from synthetic ingredients it is very expensive. People at risk from malaria are usually given artemisinin-based drugs with cheaper synthetic drugs. The treatments are called artemisinin-based combination therapies (ACTs). Wormwood is found naturally in China and Vietnam, but has been grown in Tanzania and Kenya since the 1990s as the climate is ideal and the incidence of malaria is high. Since 2005, plantations of a new, high-yielding form of Artemisia have been grown, with the support of the World Health Organisation and the African pharmaceutical company Botanical Extracts EPZ, to enable larger quantities of the active ingredient to be harvested. This has had a significant human impact in East Africa. In 2007, over 6,500 farmers grew wormwood for Botanical Extracts. Their income from selling the wormwood is double what they would have received for producing wheat or maize on the same area of land.

Malaria is a preventable and curable disease. However, in some countries over a quarter of the population have malaria. The World Health Organisation estimates that about half of the world's population is at risk from the disease, particularly in LDCs.

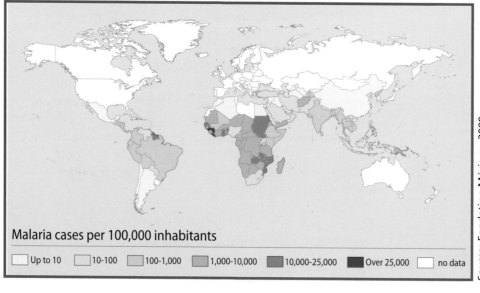

Malaria cases per 100,000 inhabitants

Up to 10 | 10-100 | 100-1,000 | 1,000-10,000 | 10,000-25,000 | Over 25,000 | no data

Source: Fondation Mérieux, 2009

Vulnerable people

The very young and old are the most susceptible to disease, and malaria is responsible for approximately one in every five childhood deaths globally. Pregnant women and their unborn children are also vulnerable to the effects of malaria. It is a major global cause of still birth, but also low birth weight and maternal anaemia, which can weaken mothers and make them more prone to illness. Apart from medicines, the other way of preventing the disease is to use mosquito nets impregnated with insecticide, so the insects cannot bite people. However, not all family members sleep under the nets. The World Health Organisation's malaria surveys in 18 African countries, in 2006–07, revealed that 34 per cent of households owned impregnated nets but only 23 per cent of children under-five slept under the nets. In most households, the head of the family, usually a man, sleeps under the net.

Combined strategies

In 1998, a global initiative was started with the aim of ending all malarial deaths by 2015. Roll Back Malaria (RBM) uses around US$3 billion-funding from the United Nations Global Fund, the World Bank and the Bill & Melinda Gates Foundation. It draws upon the expertise of governments in poor, malaria-affected countries and research institutes such as the Royal Tropical Institute, and private partners including pharmaceutical companies. RBM involves control,

Giving out long-lasting, insecticide-impregnated mosquito nets to people in malarious zones is not enough. To better control the spread of the disease, as part of a combined strategy against malaria, health workers in Ethiopia demonstrate how to use nets correctly to reduce the risk of mosquito bites.

elimination and research. Two ways in which RBM is trying to control the spread of the disease are by making the chemicals on mosquito nets last longer, using the expertise of the German pharmaceutical company Bayer, and making quick blood tests to detect malaria cheaper and more widely available. This will prevent people with fevers from other causes being treated with antimalarials. Using medicines and controls has eliminated malaria in several countries, including the United Arab Emirates, since 2007. There is also research being carried out to create better medicines to treat the disease. These include the development, manufacture and distribution of cheaper ACTs by the pharmaceutical TNC Sanofi-Aventis.

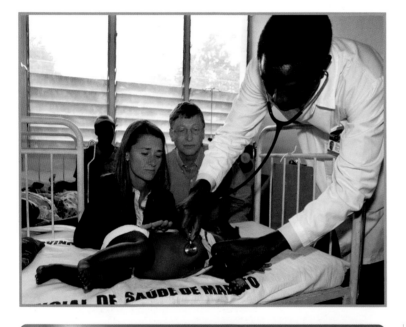

The billionaire Bill Gates and his wife Melinda visit a young patient suffering from malaria in Mozambique. Their foundation has donated hundreds of millions of dollars to fund research into malaria cures and better treatment strategies for children.

SPOTLIGHT

Access to ACTs

The most effective antimalarials are ACTs (see page 31), but in 2007 only 3 per cent of children in LDCs were receiving the ACTs they needed. One reason is that they are more expensive than other antimalarials, so the poorest countries generally have to rely on charities such as MSF to buy ACTs from pharmaceutical companies. Even when a country has ACTs, there may not be enough to go round. For example, in Sierra Leone only one-third of children get ACTs to treat one episode of malarial fever, even though they may suffer from four episodes a year. In some places, such as Mali, people rarely visit clinics as they cannot afford treatments. Even when a clinic has free ACTs to give out, malaria sufferers may not seek help.

The vaccine problem

A key aim of RBM is to develop a malaria vaccine by 2015. The problem with creating a vaccine against Plasmodium, unlike vaccines against many viruses or bacteria, is that the parasite cannot easily be grown in a laboratory. The Plasmodium that causes human malaria cannot cause it in tissue samples or in laboratory animals, so there is not a safe way to test vaccines without giving human volunteers malaria. What is more, it is hard to make people immune to malaria as the parasite can hide in body cells and avoid attack by the immune system.

The current drive to develop a vaccine came when the disease's resistance to chemicals in the 1970s onwards caused one-third of US peacekeeping troops stationed in Somalia in 1992–4 to contract malaria. The Walter Reed Army Institute of Research, in Maryland, USA, is still one of the leading malaria vaccine research laboratories. It was here that researchers found that an experimental vaccine called Mosquirix worked on soldier volunteers with malaria.

American and international troops entered Somalia in 1992 to provide aid against famine and ease violence caused by civil war. Their exposure to malaria prompted new research into vaccines to combat the disease.

The new hope for eliminating malaria

In the 21st century, many drug companies have begun to see the value of vaccines in general – partly because they cannot be copied as easily as other treatments and therefore generate more money. GlaxoSmithKline teamed up with the PATH Malaria Vaccine Initiative, part of RBM, to develop the vaccine RTS,S, based on Mosquirix. Many pharmaceutical TNCs have made global commitments to help eradicate killer diseases through initiatives such as this. Their expertise and facilities are invaluable for RBM. But the involvement also helps to raise their global profile and could make it more likely for them to make money from RTS,S if it proves successful and is widely used. In addition, the skills they develop may help GlaxoSmithKline to develop vaccines against other diseases.

GlaxoSmithKline's trials of RTS,S have already produced promising results. In 2008, trials carried out in Tanzania and Kenya on 16,000 babies, at a cost of US$100 million to RBM, halved the number of 5–17-month-old babies with severe malaria, compared with babies not given the vaccine. The vaccine could be available by 2015 if approved by the European licensing authority and WHO. However, the eventual hope is to develop an even better vaccine with 80 per cent protection against severe disease and death, for with one course lastsing over four years. There are currently just over 40 vaccines in development by different companies and one of these could be the new hope against malaria.

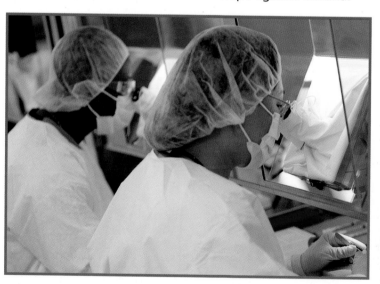

Research scientists extract Plasmodium from mosquitoes in a laboratory, for use in producing a malaria vaccine.

PERSPECTIVES FOR DEBATE

"Even a partially effective [malaria] vaccine has the potential to save hundreds of thousands of lives."

Christian Loucq, director of the PATH Malaria Vaccine Initiative, 2008

"This new research is positive but it doesn't change our message – countries still need to modify their strategies, especially in prevention and treatment. We're hopeful a vaccine could be part of a holistic approach to malaria control, as a way to reduce the severity of malaria attacks."

Boi-Betty Udom, Roll Back Malaria partnership facilitator, 2008

Making drugs in India: what are the costs?

CASE STUDY UNCOVERED

India is an LDC that is rising in wealth and global importance. Much of this has to do with the growth of the pharmaceutical industry there. However, although the industry is having many positive impacts on the country, it is also causing environmental and social problems for many poor people in places where factories are located.

Booming industry

The pharmaceutical industry is booming in India. The country not only supplies its own citizens with most of the medicines they need, but also exports drugs abroad. In 2008, India's pharmaceutical sales to the rest of the world made around US$2.5 billion, and this is expected to more than double by 2010. The money comes mostly from generic medicines – for example, India supplies most generic antibiotics used in the USA – and active ingredients that other manufacturers can use in their products. Globalised companies outsource work to India, just as they do in the IT industry. Most big foreign pharmaceutical TNCs have several offices in India, coordinating manufacture across the country. However, there are also about 20,000 Indian pharmaceutical companies employing around 500,000 people. These include big companies such as Ranbaxy Laboratories, which makes generics for the global market in factories not only in India but also in Nigeria, Vietnam and other countries. In addition, scientific expertise in India is growing fast and increasingly providing innovation and ideas for pharmaceutical companies worldwide. Each year, Indian universities produce about 130,000 graduates with master's degrees or PhDs in chemistry.

In India, between 1970 and 2004, the dominance of products sold by pharmaceutical TNCs over those sold by Indian drug companies reversed. The domestic industry in India grew during a period of rapid development in industry, technology and wealth.

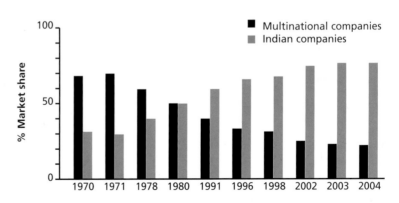

How India's pharmaceuticals market is divided

■ Multinational companies
■ Indian companies

% Market share

100 — ... 50 — ... 0 —

1970 1971 1978 1980 1991 1996 1998 2002 2003 2004

Centre of the industry

Around 40 per cent of India's pharmaceutical production happens along a 30-kilometre arc of the Patancheru region in the state of Andhra Pradesh. The industry grew in Patancheru in the 1970s, owing to a good water supply, space and the area's proximity to Hyderabad, the fifth-largest city in India. Hyderabad is a major market for drug sales and also a centre of the IT industry, which has had a significant impact on online sales of generics. Andhra Pradesh is known as the 'Bulk Drug Capital of India', and this single state contributes one-third of the combined turnover of Indian pharmaceutical companies.

SPOTLIGHT

Signs of pharmaceutical wealth

The positive impacts of the pharmaceutical industry in India are widespread. Many colleges and universities are educating future workers for the industry. For example, in 2007, the Jawaharlal Nehru Technological University became the first in Hyderabad to offer a pharmacy education master's degree. The industry has also brought wealth to the region. During 2006–07, before the global economic slowdown began, property prices in the city tripled and the number of US$1 million properties rose. Sales of cars to pharmaceutical workers contributed to a rise in this market of 30 per cent. Other trends in shopping included higher sales in luxury clothes and jewellery.

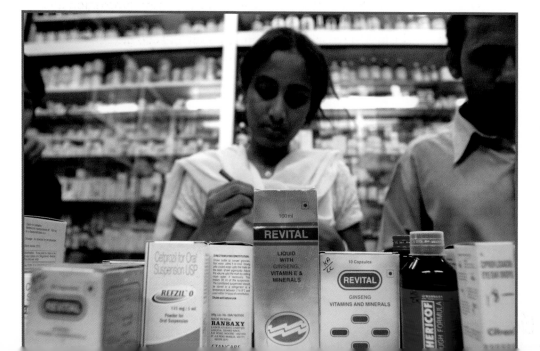

Staff check stocks of Ranbaxy medicines at a pharmacy in Mumbai. India's massive population provides an expanding market for pharmaceutical products, many made in within its borders.

Cutting corners?

There are several reasons why it is cheaper for Western pharmaceutical companies to manufacture in India than in most MDCs. There is a large workforce with high technical skills but with lower expectations of wages than in MDCs. Also, regulation of the industry is not so strongly enforced in India as it is in many MDCs. A study of quality inspections of pharmaceutical factories revealed 1,200 inspections of US drug factories compared with just 32 in India during the same period. However, many Indian factories make medicines at just as high standards as those in MDCs. For example, in 2007 Aurobindo pharmaceuticals from Patancheru in Andhra Pradesh gained a prestigious certificate of Good Manufacturing Practice from the US Medical Health Regulatory Authority, following successful inspections by both WHO and the FDA.

Skilled Indian technicians work in the laboratory of an Indian pharmaceutical company in Mumbai.

Drug testing

Pharmaceutical companies in MDCs have a problem testing
their drugs because there are few volunteers who will take
the risk of trying new, largely unproven treatments. That
is why companies look to countries such as India to find
volunteers. The TNC Quintiles, based in North Carolina, USA,
is a company that specialises in organising drug trials for
pharmaceutical TNCs around the world. In India they can
enrol hundreds of volunteers for a new drug in just a few
days – far more quickly than in the USA.

The advantages of India for drug-testing companies are its
large population of poor people, with over two-thirds of the
nation living on less than US$2 a day. This means that many
people will willingly take a small payment to risk trying new,
unproven medicines. However, many volunteers are also
uneducated and do not understand that some drugs could
possibly harm or even kill them. In 2003 in Hyderabad, a
trial of a heart-attack drug resulted in six deaths. Problems
are made worse by the fact that trials are often run by
doctors paid by pharmaceutical companies to deliver results.
Some are not experienced at spotting side-effects of trial
drugs or even ignore them because they want to be able to
do more trials in future.

SPOTLIGHT

Who are the drugs for?

Is it right that Indians are putting themselves at risk to test drugs for
conditions they are unlikely to get or which they cannot afford? Many
of the drugs tested are for typical MDC problems such as diabetes
and heart disease. A 2005 trial at Sevagram hospital, in a rural part of
central India, tested a new drug on 8,000 patients with heart
problems. The drug improved the health of some patients. After the
trial, no patients could afford the treatment at £13 per day. Most
people who routinely come to Sevagram suffer from accidental
poisoning, not heart problems. The doctor in charge of testing said:
"The biggest problems around here are snakebite and insecticide
poisoning. We could really use a trial for one of those."

Pollution and disease

The production of large amounts of medicines creates a lot of polluting waste, which can cause health problems. For example, poisonous chemicals, such as toluene and chloroform, are routinely used to create the chemical reactions that form medicines, and once used they become waste. Pharmaceutical factories in Andhra Pradesh are legally required to transport hazardous waste to a Central Effluent Treatment Plant (CETP) and pay for it to be dealt with by specialist treatments or disposal. However, some companies dump the waste illegally at night, to avoid these costs. Also, the volume of waste going through the CETP means that some waste flows from the plant in treatment water that is not properly cleaned.

SPOTLIGHT

Development backfires

Up to the 1970s, Patancheru was a farming region famous for sparkling lakes and streams. People who lived here were mostly poor subsistence farmers. In 1973, the Andhra Pradesh Industrial Infrastructure Corporation was formed to promote development of industry in order to create employment. The state government bought up farmland at low prices and invested in industrial estates, of which Kazipalli in Patancheru was the biggest, and these became home to the pharmaceutical industry. With rapid development came unsafe use of chemicals and inadequate treatment of waste, and toxins including arsenic, lead and chlorine accumulated in the environment. This affected land and water so much that many farmers could no longer work. Today, the area is amongst the 22 most polluted places in India.

The groundwater in the Patancheru area is unsafe to drink as a result of pollution from pharmaceutical factories. The local farming industry has mostly shut down. Farmers can no longer grow rice plants in polluted irrigation water. Milk and meat from buffaloes and other livestock are poisoned and doctors report that people here are far sicker than average across India. A study by Greenpeace in October 2004 compared the health of 9,000 villagers in the Patancheru region with villagers in a non-industrial part of Andhra Pradesh. They found 11 times the cases of cancer, 16 times the incidence of heart disease and four times the number of birth defects in Patancheru.

> *While the 250-odd industries set up in Patancheru created about 25,000 jobs, it resulted in the displacement of more than 30,000 people due to ground water pollution. Hundreds of farmers are forced to work as casual laborers in the industries.*
>
> The *Indian Express* newspaper, 1985

This cartoon sums up the winners and losers from the rise of the pharmaceutical industry in Patancheru.

Cleaning up their act

The Indian pharmaceutical industry says that the worst pollution happened in the 1980s and 1990s, when there was less regulation, and that businesses today are much more sustainable. More companies are installing pollution control systems, such as regular testing of the water used and released again by factories. The Andhra Pradesh Pollution Control Board today keeps a look-out for illegal dumping. Air pollution has been reduced in and around the town of Kazipalli Patancheru, and clean water is now piped into all villages in the area where groundwater is unsafe. However, supplies are insufficient for all villagers' needs. They still need to use stream and river water to wash clothes or even bathe, thereby exposing themselves to the dangerous impacts of the successful local industry.

Becoming an active global citizen

What is an active global citizen? It is someone who tries, in their own small way, to make the world a better place. To become an active global citizen, you will need to get involved in decisions that others make about your life and the lives of others around the world. Consider how the world could be changed, such as improving the environment, political or social conditions for others, and seek information about the issues from a wide variety of sources. Then go public by presenting your arguments to others, from friends and local groups to national politicians and global organisations.

In your life

Hopefully this book has helped you to think about your actions as a user of pharmaceutical products. The pharmaceutical industry is massive, rich and powerful, with complex interdependencies between people, cultures and nations. So how can you get to grips with the important issues involved?

Know your medicines. Consider your family's global impact through the pharmaceutical industry. Start by looking at the pharmaceutical products in your home. Which pharmaceutical company created them? Are they patented brands or generics? In which country were they made? What are the possible side-effects? Find out information from the labels but also from company websites. If you need to know more, ask the companies directly.

Question the products. We all know about the products of the pharmaceutical industry from adverts in newspapers, magazines and on TV. How do drug companies create a need for their products using adverts? Is an expensive meltable headache caplet really an improvement on a cheaper generic pill, or is this a way to make us spend more? Scratch away at the surface of what the industry wants you to see and investigate what lies beneath. Find out about instances when drug companies have made inaccurate claims about what they make, or hidden evidence about the possible bad effects of their products.

Inform yourself. Go to any drug company website and they will give a very positive impression of their products, their commitment to employees, care for the environment and other aspects. There's a list of many top companies, with links to their websites, at: http://www.biopsychiatry.com/drugcompanies.
To get an idea of more critical points of view about the pharmaceutical industry, check out:
• the pharmaceuticals section of the CorpWatch website at http://www.corpwatch.org/section.php?id=122
• the links at the foot of the biopsychiatry.com website.

Key terms for internet searches

Type these terms into a search engine on the internet and see what results you get. How many hits appear? Are the websites from around the world, and are there any sources that surprise you?

- World Health Organisation
- Generic medicines
- Counterfeit medicines
- Globalisation and the pharmaceutical industry
- China's growing pharmaceutical market
- Traditional medicines
- Malaria vaccine

- South Africa HIV/AIDS
- ARVs Africa
- Drug resistance
- Drug safety
- Global drug trials
- Animal testing
- Personalised medicines
- Medical tourism
- Big pharma

Data watch

Keep on top of global statistics by visiting these thought-provoking websites.

http://www.worldmapper.org
What is different about the maps on this site is that countries and regions are distorted according to the data. Here are a few maps to explore: 389) Malaria deaths; 374) HIV/AIDS deaths; 451) Cardiovascular (heart and blood vessel) disease; 154) Living on up to $10; and 158) Living on over $200.

http://www.globalpolicy.org/globaliz/charts/index
According to the Global Policy Forum, 'Globalisation creates new markets and wealth, even as it causes widespread suffering, disorder, and unrest. It is both a source of repression and a catalyst for global movements of social justice and emancipation.' On this page you can find links to data in tables and charts that show changes in technology, demographics and culture as a result of globalisation.

http://www.abpi.org.uk/statistics/intro.asp
The Association of the British Pharmaceutical Industry hosts a very useful statistics and facts page with links to data on the global and UK pharmaceutical industry. Look for:
- information about the changes over the last few decades in NHS spending per person in the UK
- comparisons between the value of pharmaceutical exports and imports in different countries.
This information was compiled from a UK perspective. Can you locate an equivalent site that focuses on the US pharmaceutical industry?

http://www.worldometers.info
Ever wanted to see the rate at which data such as world population or the number of internet users change? This website has up-to-the-minute information! See the health section for figures on malaria and HIV/AIDS.

Topic web

Use this topic web to discover the themes and ideas in subjects that are related to the pharmaceutical industry.

Geography
Polluted groundwater is a growing global problem, caused in part by waste from industry, including pharmaceuticals. Create a global map of groundwater contamination and assess the impacts of water pollution on agriculture and population.

Citizenship
Find out the contrasting points of view about animal testing of drugs, from the bombing of laboratories by animal rights activists to the globally successful products that have relied on testing during their creation, and the viability of alternatives to animal tests. What is your own opinion of drug testing based on these pros and cons?

English
Create an advert that persuades doctors to buy a pharmaceutical product made by your company. Your task is to stress the need for your product and its benefits, backing it up with results from clinical trials. You will need to be honest about any side-effects, too. How can you use persuasive language to make readers focus on the pros and not the cons?

The Pharmaceutical Industry

Maths
The pharmaceutical industry seeks to offer cures to the many health problems caused by being overweight. Compare data on the health indicator BMI/Overweight/Obesity (BMI, or body-mass index, is the ratio of weight to height) between countries at http://www.who.int/infobase/comparestart.aspx. Find out those countries' populations and calculate how many people are likely to be obese in each.

Science
Aspirin is often described as a wonder-drug that can help people with many different conditions. Find out about the chemistry of aspirin, how it is made, how it works and what its side-effects can be.

ICT
Create a powerpoint presentation for a made-up condition associated with using mobile phones, such as mobilosis or textfingeritis. You should create a master slide with a logo, title and menu linking to subsequent slides. Then create different slides explaining the impacts of the condition, its treatability or cure and its global distribution. Include pictures of your own or downloaded from the internet.

History
Research the history of penicillin, from its use in World War II to eradicating smallpox. How did these events affect the growth of drugs companies?

Glossary

active ingredient A substance in a product, such as a medicine, that performs the main function of that product.

anti-depressant Medication that stimulates the mood of a depressed patient.

antimalarial A drug normally used to treat malaria.

antiretroviral drugs (ARVs) A type of medication used to treat infections by retroviruses, most commonly HIV.

brand A symbol, mark or quality that characterises a product. It has been called 'a product's personality'.

chemotherapy Treatment of cancer with chemicals (drugs) formulated to kill cancer cells and stop them from growing.

clinical trial Testing a treatment on human subjects to evaluate its safety and effectiveness.

complementary medicine Traditional health practices that involve natural medicines, spiritual therapies and other alternative remedies.

condition An illness, disease or other medical problem.

counterfeit drug A fake or imitation pharmaceutical product made to mimic an original product in order to deceive purchasers.

diversification Establishing new products and markets, sometimes outside normal areas of business, to increase sales.

generic drug A medicine with an active ingredient that is no longer protected by a patent, which may be produced by any manufacturer and is generally cheaper than the original.

global warming The average global temperature rise that most scientists agree is caused by increases in greenhouse gases such as carbon dioxide, released largely by human machines, in the atmosphere.

Gross domestic product (GDP) The value of all goods and services produced by a country in a single year.

health insurance Financial protection against medical care costs.

HIV/AIDS HIV is a virus that weakens the immune system. AIDS is a set of symptoms and infections that may result from lack of immunity caused by HIV.

immune system The body's defence system against infections, which includes white blood cells, barriers such as the skin and organs including the bone marrow and spleen.

infrastructure The systems that support a country such as roads, water supply, waste, power supply, access to shops and other resources.

insulin A hormone that regulates blood sugar levels. Diabetics take insulin as their bodies cannot make enough.

interdependent When organisations, industries or individuals are mutually dependent on each other to make something work.

less developed countries (LDCs) Countries that have a lower income and poorer standards in health, nutrition, education and industry than more developed countries (MDCs).

media All means of providing or communicating information to the public, including radio, the internet, television, mobile phones and newspapers.

migrate To move from one country or region to settle in another.

more developed countries (MDCs) Countries that have a higher income and better standards in health, nutrition, education and industry than less developed countries (LDCs).

patent An exclusive right to a product or process that provides a new way of doing something. When patents expire, anyone may have access to the idea.

postcode prescribing Unequal access to medicines in different regions, because of costs or healthcare infrastructure.

side-effect An effect of a drug or other therapy on tissues or organs, which is in addition to the desired therapeutic effect.

subsidies Payments made to an industry by its government.

sustainable Able to be maintained at a steady level for a long time, without causing environmental or social harm.

transfusion Replacing blood or blood components that someone has lost in surgery, through an accident or as a result of medical treatment.

transnational company (TNC) A company that operates across several nations.

vaccine A treatment that is given to produce or increase immunity, or resistance, to a particular disease.

World Health Organisation (WHO) An organisation of the United Nations, concerned with worldwide public health.

Index

Global Industries Uncovered

Contents of titles in the series:

WAYLAND